Adventures with Leo

Overcoming Fears

By Leslie K. Lang

ISBN: 979-8-8692-1629-8
Printed in the United States of America
Published by Bookmarketeers.com

Dedication Page

I dedicate this book to my dad. He was the most fearless man I have ever known. He instilled bravery in me to go out into this world and make my life my own and I am forever grateful for his belief in me. He encouraged me to live my life to the fullest and gave me a solid foundation for being a good person in the process.I miss his guidance in my life.

I also dedicate this book to my husband, who stepped in and became the biggest source of support and encouragement in my adult life and has never let me believe there is anything I can't do if I set my mind to it. He is a true inspiration and absolutely brilliant.

Hi there! My name is Leo. I am a puppy, and I want to share my adventures with you. Come join me and be my friend as you read about all the things that make my life so fun and adventurous. I want to start with the beginning, so here we go.

The first few weeks of my life my brother's,
sister's and I stayed close to our mama,she was
so loving and kind.We mainly slept and drank
milk and it felt very safe.We would all curl up
together and sleep.it was so warm and nice.

What person's or place's makes you feel safe and loved?
Can you count how many puppies are in the picture?
How many are brown and how many are yellow?

After a few weeks the people that we lived with started taking all of us puppies somewhere away from our mama. This made me sad, and one day it was me and one of my brothers that got taken away. We looked at each other with sad eyes, I wanted to cry. We were scared to be away from our mama and we didn't know where we were going.

Has anything new ever made you scared?

It is okay to be scared but when you are, talk to the people you love so they can help you deal with your feelings in a good way. My brother and I were there for each other.

When we got to the new house it was very different, but these people were nice too. I was so glad to have my brother with me. These people had a small back yard with lots of plants. They had big dogs that liked to play so we had new friends to play with. We ran and played with the toys outside. I came across some green things that looked like big plants.

I took a bite of one and my tongue was hurting because it was hot, then I started itching all over and my tummy looked red. The people noticed and gave me some medicine that made me feel better. I didn't do that again!

Can you find the green pepper plant in the picture?
Do you know what the veggies are in their garden?

I started getting use to
the new house, but after a
few days my brother was
picked up by some new
people and I was alone.
I knew these people were
nice, but I was scared and
missed my family.

The other dogs tried
to cheer me up and told
me it would be okay and
a special family would
come find me and make
me their puppy.

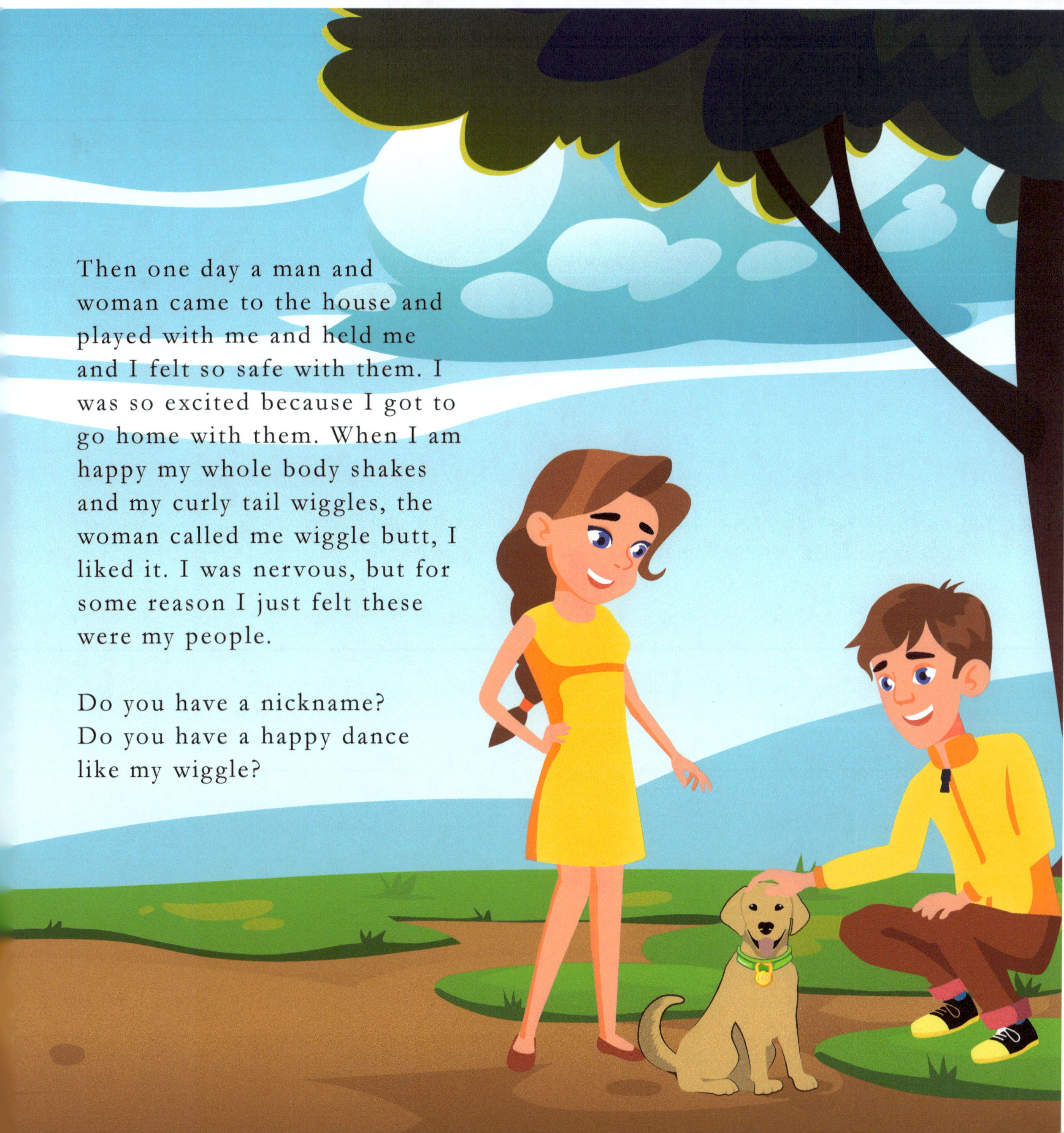

Then one day a man and woman came to the house and played with me and held me and I felt so safe with them. I was so excited because I got to go home with them. When I am happy my whole body shakes and my curly tail wiggles, the woman called me wiggle butt, I liked it. I was nervous, but for some reason I just felt these were my people.

Do you have a nickname?
Do you have a happy dance like my wiggle?

On the way home they stopped at a place that had special treats for puppies like me and it was white and sweet and served in a cup. I licked the cup clean and then licked off what I had gotten on my nose. It was so good!!

Can you find the cup of whip cream in the picture?
Do you have a favorite sweet treat?

When I got to the house that would be my home, I explored the big backyard that they had it was just for me! I discovered lots of other animals. I played with these things that looked like sticks and my people called them stick bugs. I played with this green bug that hopped I chased flying things that had wings. and these pretty small flying things. There was a family of small animals with cute white tails, they were faster than me and I am pretty fast.

How many animals do you see in the pictures?
What is your favorite animal?

There were these big black and brown animals behind our back yard. I was a little scared of them at first, but they were very nice to me and mooed at me.

Do you know what kind of animal this is?

The dogs next door barked a lot at me at first, but they soon became my friends. Their names are Cooper and Dolly. Cooper kind of likes to do his own thing, but Dolly and I love to run together and we meet at the back of the fence and explore.

What colors are Dolly and Cooper? If you have a best friend, what do you like to do for fun with them?

My people taught me how to play ball. They throw the ball way out in the yard and I run really fast and bring it back. I like to try to play keep away with them. I don't think they like that very much, but it is fun for me.

Do you have fun games you like to play with your family? What colors are the balls I am playing with in the picture?

I have really nice people, their names are Rich and Les, but I have decided they will be my mama and daddy. Oh and when my people met me my name was Starbuck and my people didn't feel that name fit me, so they both agreed that Leo was a much better name for me. I really like it!!

Why did your parent's give you the name they gave you?

Mama and daddy give me lots of treats and toys and show me so much love. At nighttime I get sleepy and lay on the couch with them. When it is time for bed I run to my bed and my mama brings me my bedtime bones, it helps me sleep.

Can you count how many little bones she brings me?
What color is my dog bed that I sleep on?

I was so scared when I was taken from my home, but my new home with my new mama and daddy makes me feel safe and loved. Even though I was scared, I was strong and didn't let my fear keep me from giving my new home a chance. I know you can see how happy I am in the picture with my mama and daddy.
They are the best!!!
Remember, when you are scared, it is important to talk to the family you love so they can help you. New things in life can be scary, but your people can teach you how to cope with those fears and be okay.
I hope you will join me on my next adventure!

Discussion Page

Leo would like you and your family to have time to discuss
what you learned from this book.

What are some things that make you scared or fearful?

What do your loved ones do when they are scared or fearful?

Do new things in your life sometimes make you afraid?

What is something that you really want to do but
you are afraid to do it?

Do you have something special that makes you feel better
when you are nervous, like a toy, stuffed animal, or a friend?

Tell your parents or family if you are nervous or sad and
struggling so they can help you.

Leo would like you to know that it is perfectly normal to
be fearful or afraid of things, but you can't let that stop
you from being around new people or trying new things.
He wants you to have the best life a little girl or boy can have,
so he wants you to develop healthy ways to deal with those
fears and push past them to have the best life you can have.

Until our next adventure!

LEO'S FUTURE LESSONS TO LEARN

- KINDNESS
- LEADERSHIP
- HUMILITY
- FRIENDSHIP
- FORGIVENESS
- COMMUNICATION
- PROBLEM SOLVING
- INDEPENDENCE
- UNCONDITIONAL LOVE

About The Author

The author has been a Licensed Professional Counselor for 20 years. Leslie has seen many changes in our society and in people over the course of this time and is truly concerned about the foundation of children's character. We live in a fast-paced society with excessive use of technology, And She is passionate about protecting children's futures. Her biggest concern is parent's having a lack of influence in the development of their children. Leslie works with people daily who are coping with the negative impact of people neglecting, avoiding, abusing, or abandoning them in their lives and she gets the privilege of helping them heal, but she believes as a society, we can do better and it starts with being a support to our kids and a foundation for their well- being. Leslie hopes this book series encourages parents to read these books with their children. have open conversations and make this the start of good communication skills. This will hopefully lead to open emotional interaction as well as fun learning. We hope that you and your family enjoy going on adventures with Leo as much as we do!

About Leo

In case you are wondering. Leo is a real dog. We adopted him from Austin Pets Alive in Austin, Texas, in June 2021. He is an amazing mix! We did testing on him and let's just say he has about 7 different breeds of dog in him, but they said he is about 26% super mutt and we like that. He is the sweetest, kindest, and most loyal dog we have ever owned. All of the books in this series are based on true events and the wonderful mischief he gets into. We hope you enjoy reading about Leo as much as we enjoy having him as our dog.

Leo loves answering questions and learning about new people. Send him an email so he can do his wiggle butt dance for us! **AdventureswithLeo1@gmail.com**

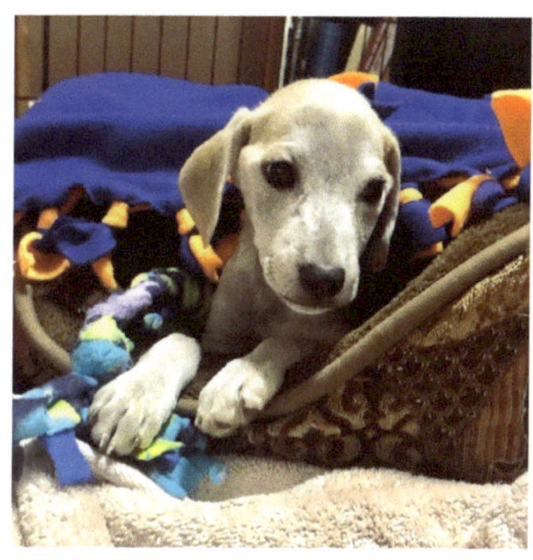
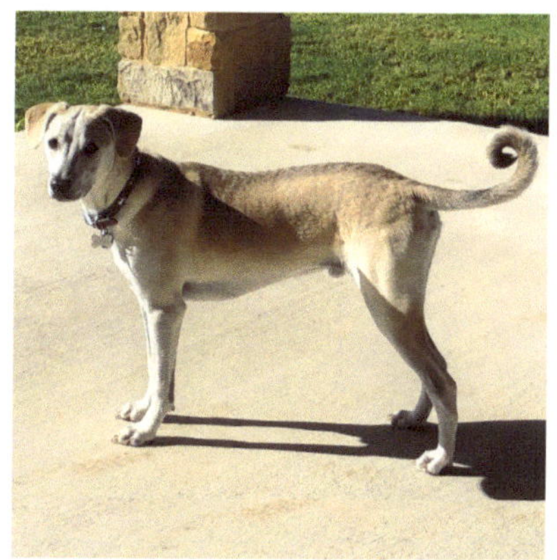